Original title:
The Myth of the Mossy Oak

Copyright © 2025 Creative Arts Management OÜ
All rights reserved.

Author: Evelyn Hartman
ISBN HARDBACK: 978-1-80567-413-9
ISBN PAPERBACK: 978-1-80567-712-3

Shadows Among the Foliage

Underneath the leafy green,
A squirrel plots, oh what a scene!
He hoards his acorns, such a thief,
In a world where nuts bring disbelief.

Laughter echoes in the breeze,
As branches dance with playful ease.
The shadows wink, they know the jest,
In a forest full of woodsy quests.

The Voice of Times Past

Whispers float through the knotted bark,
Of tales that light the forest dark.
A chipmunk chuckles, a wise old sage,
Spouting secrets from some distant age.

The toadstools giggle, mushrooms sway,
In the memories of yesterday.
A chorus hums, the leaves applaud,
For the past is fun, though it seems odd.

Home of the Timeless Wanderers

In the nook of knobbly roots,
Reside the critters in their suits.
They toast to time with leafy tea,
In a cozy den, just you and me.

The owls debate on who knows best,
While rabbits play a guessing jest.
A party grows beneath the sun,
Where every critter's just here for fun.

Birth of a Chestnut Dream

From the ground, a sprout does peak,
A chestnut thinks, 'I'm quite unique!'
"I'll be the tallest, just you wait,"
But winds of humor are his fate.

As time rolls on, he tumbles down,
With giggles shared across the town.
A nutty tale, a dream so sweet,
In cozy corners, laughter's complete.

Echoes of the Olden Woods

In the woods where whispers play,
Squirrels hold a dance today.
With acorn hats and tiny shoes,
They jive beneath the dappled hues.

Old stumps tell tales of times gone by,
While owls chuckle in the sky.
Frogs in toadstools stage a show,
As daisies join in with a glow.

Beneath the Bark

Beneath the bark, a secret crew,
With worms in hats and a grand view.
Ants march in line, a tiny parade,
While crickets tune up for a serenade.

Mice in scarves pop out to chew,
On twigs that look like fancy stew.
They gossip merrily, while badgers sleep,
In a world so silly, no secrets keep.

Guardians of the Gnarled Roots

Guardians of roots, all bent and wise,
Crickets croon under moonlit skies.
Bats play tag, oh what a sight,
While raccoons giggle, alive at night.

Each twist and turn holds laughter's song,
The forest echoes, all night long.
With squirrels leaping, a playful dance,
They bop and weave in a merry prance.

Serpents Among the Leaves

Serpents twist in leafy beds,
Wearing hats made of daisies' heads.
They wiggle and giggle, quite the scene,
Playing hide and seek, so keen.

Lizards lounge, sunbathing bright,
While chipmunks scurry to alight.
With laughter echoing through the glade,
In a playful world, no need for shade.

Dreams in Orange and Emerald

In the woods where squirrels dance,
Leaves wear hats, the deer take a chance.
Underneath the glowing moon,
Frogs croak out a silly tune.

Owls crack jokes at midnight's call,
While sleeping bears just take a fall.
Raccoons wear masks, they've got flair,
As trees whisper secrets in the air.

Stories From the Elder Part of the Woods

Mighty pines share a gossip spree,
About a raccoon who climbed a tree.
A fox played dress-up, oh what a sight,
In a tutu made of leaves, shining bright.

The rabbits tell tales of great mishaps,
Like when they lost their way through the maps.
They giggle as the fox trips in style,
Dancing through brambles with a big smile.

Secrets Beneath the Twisted Canopy

Under the leaves, a party takes place,
Where worms wear ribbons, it's no disgrace.
A snail sings ballads, slow yet grand,
While ants join in, forming a band.

Mice trade stories with plenty of cheese,
About the sunshine, the buzzing bees.
Beneath the roots, laughter flows wide,
As nature joins in for the fun ride.

A Tribute to the Ancient Guardian

An old tree stands with branches so wide,
With a grin on its face, it opens wide.
Squirrels gather, they race up the bark,
Playing hide and seek until it's dark.

Each knot in its trunk tells a silly lore,
Of woodland parties and dances galore.
As night settles in with stars that twinkle,
The tree laughs softly, feeling quite sprightly.

Oaths of the Old Forest

In the shadows, squirrels plot,
As they gather acorns a lot.
Whispered vows in the breeze,
With giggles hidden in the trees.

Deer in tuxedos prance with glee,
Sipping dew like fine chamomile tea.
Branches chuckle, leaves dance low,
Each twig's a comedian, don't you know?

Rabbits in top hats and capes,
Spin tales of forest escapes.
Beneath the boughs, mischief brews,
Nature's court, with oddball crews.

In this old grove, laughter reigns,
Where even fungus wears fun chains.
Mirth entwined in every nook,
The woods are best with a funny book.

The Keeper of Nature's Secrets

The wise old owl wears glasses thick,
His puns are sharp, his timing quick.
Hooting riddles from his perch,
He runs the best tree-top church.

Raccoons in robes make midnight feasts,
Telling tall tales like nature's beasts.
With giggly hiccups from their cups,
The forest echoes with joyful ups.

The wily fox winks at the crowd,
Making shadows dance, oh-so-proud.
With a flair for the dramatic, he sways,
Chasing away the gloomy days.

Through the thickets, laughter darts,
In secret chambers and leafy carts.
Nature's jester, bright and keen,
In a world where smiles are evergreen.

Mysteries of the Ancient Woodland

Beneath the bark, secrets hide,
From chuckling gnomes, we cannot bide.
Mossy knolls, with clues entwined,
Whispered giggles in the pines.

The ancient tree boasts tales so grand,
With roots that weave like a band.
Bugs wearing hats, a party spread,
Not a boring branch to dread.

Mushrooms tease with colors bright,
Each one dressed for a wild night.
Squirrels debating wise old lore,
Who knew the woods could be such a score?

Amidst the hush, the woodland croons,
As critters dance to goofy tunes.
The ancient trees, with wisdom old,
List their secrets, in jest retold.

A Testament of Timber

Beneath the timbered giants tall,
Lies a court where creatures sprawl.
In their woodsy conference hall,
Jokes and jests, all to enthrall.

Bears in slippers share sweet tea,
Expanding their feline family tree.
While raccoons juggle with such flair,
A round of applause fills the air.

The creaky branches join delight,
With snap-crackle pops under moonlight.
Every root holds a punchline tight,
In this testament, all's just right.

So come, my friend, and take a look,
A logging legacy, but not a book.
In laughter's arms, the forest beams,
With timber tales and funny dreams.

The Enchanted Rooted Realm

In a land where trees wear hats,
And critters hum like jazz.
A squirrel with a monocle chats,
While dancing on a soft green grass.

The acorns giggle and bob,
As the light winds weave a song.
Even mushrooms join the mob,
Frolicking all night long.

Tales Carved in Bark and Bone

There's a chipmunk with a tale,
Of walnuts lost in vain.
He swears it's no fairy tale,
But his bark is full of grain.

Old trees gossip with a grin,
Rumors rise like misty air.
Legends grow from marks within,
As owls laugh without a care.

Moonlight on Moss-Covered Roots

Underneath the moon's bright eye,
The roots are telling jokes.
A nightingale begins to fly,
And bumps into some folks.

The moss giggles, soft and green,
As shadows start to dance.
A lizard joins the silly scene,
With moves that make us prance.

Spirits of the Verdant Realm

The spirits wear flowered crowns,
Tickling leaves and making cheer.
They surf the breezes, layin' down,
A trail of laughter near.

With every rustle, there's a wink,
A jester in the barked embrace.
They mix up acorns with a drink,
And toast each silly face.

Songs of the Silent Trunk

In whispers low, the branches sigh,
They tell of acorns that once flew high.
A squirrel's concert—a wobbly play,
Dancing leaves spin, come join the fray.

With limbs outstretched, the trunk stands proud,
It groans as critters scurry, loud.
A party here beneath the bark,
Where laughter echoes from dawn till dark.

The Dance of the Forest Floor

The mushrooms twirl, the ferns all sway,
To the tunes of wind, they leap and play.
A rabbit hops, a deer prances near,
In this forest, there's nothing to fear.

With shadows long and laughter bright,
Every creature finds pure delight.
A beetle spins, rolls with a twist,
In their jig, no moment is missed.

Beneath the Dappled Sun

Sunlight dapples on the ground,
While sleepy critters gather round.
A turtle's slow shuffle, a snail's quick race,
Every nook holds a silly face.

The shadows laugh, the light does tease,
As bumblebees buzz just as they please.
A chorus of frogs joins in the cheer,
Under the canopy, fun is near.

Life Among the Elder Trees

Old trunks lean in with tales to share,
Of world adventures, from here to there.
Chipper birds gossip about the breeze,
While raccoons plan their nightly tease.

The wise old owl hoots on his perch,
As critters gather for the nightly search.
In this meadow of giggles and grins,
Every story here, together begins.

Beneath the Veil of Verdure

In the woods where whispers play,
An acorn fell, or so they say.
It bounced and rolled, then found its throne,
Now it claims the shady zone.

Squirrels run a silly race,
Chasing tails at a frantic pace.
A napping fox grins through his dreams,
Of nutty feasts and pie-filled schemes.

Reverie in the Bark

Old tree trunks wear a wrinkled grin,
With gossip swirling in the wind.
A wise old owl hoots with delight,
As branches sway and dance at night.

The woodpecker plays his daily tune,
Knocking rhythm like a cartoon.
"Hey, who's that making such a ruckus?"
"Just me!" he laughs, "No need for fuss!"

The Soul of the Swaying Branch

In a breeze, the branches sway,
A dance party in shades of gray.
Leaves laugh and gossip, twist and twirl,
Nature's laughter makes hearts whirl.

A caterpillar in a top hat prances,
Dreaming big of bold romances.
He shimmies past the spider's net,
"What a splendid stage we've all just met!"

Silhouettes Against the Setting Sun

As day recedes, the shadows stretch,
A chorus of critters in silhouette.
The bunnies dance in shadowed glee,
While crickets play their symphony.

A strange old frog starts to croon,
Singing loudly to the moon.
"Oh, don't forget your silly hats!"
"Let's have a ball!" the firefly chats.

Whispers Beneath the Canopy

In the shade of the old tree, leaves giggle and sway,
Squirrels tell tales of nuts stored away.
Beneath the broad branches, shadows dance light,
While critters plot mischief 'til well after night.

The raccoons convene for their weekly chat,
Discussing grand heists for a late-night snack.
The wise old owl hoots, 'You're all quite absurd!'
But they just roll their eyes, not caring nor stirred.

A woodpecker knocks on a trunk for a tune,
While rabbits race past, with nary a swoon.
The laughter cascades like drops from the skies,
As the trees keep their secrets, while everyone spies.

So come grab a seat, join the rowdy crew,
In the heart of the forest, where laughter is true.
Nature's great stage, with humor so bright,
Under the canopy, it's pure delight.

Legends Wrapped in Green

Underneath twisted roots, where the stories unfold,
Frogs croak the tales of treasures untold.
Beneath leafy arches, they plot and they scheme,
A frog named Steve dreams a grand ice cream.

The fireflies flicker, like stars made of gold,
As mice host a banquet with cheese that they mold.
The trees lean in close, with ears made of bark,
Listening in on the chirps, 'til well after dark.

Beetles in tuxedos dance round the trunk,
While turtles toast to the critters they punk.
'Rendezvous here!' they squeal in delight,
For tonight's the shared feast, under moon's silver light.

Then comes dawn's break, with a giggle and yawn,
The legends retire, but won't soon be gone.
For in every rustle, a new tale appears,
Wrapped in green laughter, through all of the years.

Secrets of the Ancient Tree

In the shade of the tree, where the whispers reside,
A squirrel named Larry is full of his pride.
He claims he once tamed a wild summer breeze,
But no one believes, not even the bees.

The ancient tree chuckles, its bark full of age,
As chipmunks recount tales that fill up the page.
One says there's a dragon who hoards acorn gold,
But everyone snickers, 'That's just getting old!'

The hedgehogs bring cupcakes, all lumpy and round,
With frosting that wobbles when set on the ground.
They dive into stories as giants of lore,
While the leaves titter softly - oh, what's in store?

As night starts to fall, there's a soft, mellow glow,
With promises kept of more tales in tow.
The ancient tree sighs, tales woven in grace,
Keeping secrets alive in this magical place.

Beneath the Boughs of Legend

Under expansive branches, a party ensues,
As fireflies dress up in their twinkling shoes.
Rabbits wear hats made of petals and leaves,
While dancing through shadows, they chuckle and weave.

Round the old stump, there's laughter and cheer,
With a fairytale fox spinning tales we hold dear.
'Once I caught starlight!' he boasts with a grin,
But they all know he's fibbing, so where to begin?

The badger, a joker, plays pranks in the dirt,
Slipping on slugs with a comical spurt.
While the wise old tortoise moves slowly with pride,
Rolling his eyes at the chaos outside.

As night wraps its curtain and the moon starts to peep,
The critters laugh softly, then drift off to sleep.
For beneath these great boughs, where the legends take flight,
There's always a whimsy, enchanting the night.

The Timeless Sentinel

Beneath the sky so wide and clear,
A tree stands tall, it holds no fear.
With acorns dropping like silly bombs,
It giggles softly, nature's charms.

Its branches wave like arms in dance,
Inviting critters for a chance.
Squirrels scatter, birds take flight,
All wonder if they'll win this fight.

The bark, a canvas of twisted tale,
With every knot, it tells a wail.
A beetle marches on a quest,
While grasshoppers play the hopscotch fest.

The roots are tangled, a maze of glee,
Playing tricks on all who see.
Nature's joker, wise and old,
Its laughter echoes, a joy untold.

Dreams of the Woodland Spirit

In twilight's whisper, creatures cheer,
A sprite appears from far and near.
With glowing wings, it starts to prance,
It turns the night into a dance.

A rabbit offers it a snack,
A carrot hat, both round and black.
The owl hoots with a funny wink,
"Is that a joke or just a drink?"

Under the leaves, they play charades,
The moonlight joins in parades.
A raccoon tries a silly pose,
While giggly vines around him close.

With laughter shared, the spirits weave,
A tapestry only they believe.
In wooded dreams, they find their joy,
A playful world, no care, no ploy.

Legends of the Knotted Limbs

Among the trees, a tale unfolds,
Of knots and twists and legends bold.
A lumberjack with no real skill,
Once thought to carve, but found a thrill.

He tripped and fell, but what a sight,
The limbs wiggled with all their might.
They told him tales of bark and leaf,
And laughed so hard, it brought him grief.

"Was that a sneeze, or just a bark?"
The trees erupted, even past dark.
With every knot, a story brewed,
Of squirrels cooking, soup stewed good.

So if you stop, take heed and glance,
You'll see the trees still share their dance.
Each twist and curl, a joyful spin,
Where laughter grows and tales begin.

Memories in Moss and Stone

In shadows deep, where moss does cling,
A frog croaks out a silly spring.
With stones like chairs beneath a dome,
They share their thoughts of a distant home.

"Did you hear about the toad that jumped,
And made the ladybug so grumped?"
The stones all chuckle, wise and round,
In quiet corners, tales abound.

The moss recalls a time so grand,
When fairies danced in wondrous band.
The lizards laughed, "What's next I ask?
A snail to join? Let's take the task!"

So when you wander, pause and peek,
These ancient friends have tales to speak.
In every rock and patch of green,
A world of laughter waits, unseen.

In the Embrace of the Elder Wood

In a forest filled with giggles,
The trees wear hats quite wide.
Squirrels dance in polka dots,
While owls strut with pride.

Beneath the boughs, a picnic spreads,
With acorns served as sweets.
A rabbit rolls a blueberry pie,
While hedgehogs play with beats.

The winds join in the laughter,
As leaves swirl in delight.
Each twig a playful storyteller,
In this charming woodland sight.

With every step, a whisper,
Of jokes from days gone by.
The elder wood holds secrets,
In each tree that reaches high.

The Quiet Majesty of the Grove

In a grove where whispers tangle,
And shadows play in jest,
A bear in boots sings show tunes,
While critters cheer the best.

With vines that twist like laughter,
And branches that sway and tease,
The squirrels tell their tall tales,
As the breeze lets out a wheeze.

Each nut is a tiny treasure,
The raccoons gather round.
In this majestic funny realm,
Joy is easily found.

The sun peeks through the branches,
Winking like a playful sprite.
In the quiet majesty,
Every day feels just right.

Shadows of the Nurtured Land

Beneath the shimm'ring lantern light,
Funny shadows prance and play.
A fox in lederhosen winks,
As night steals the day away.

With stars that sparkle blatantly,
Like diamonds in a trickster's hat,
The trees tell tales of mischief,
While frogs croak the chitchat.

In verdant patches full of glee,
A beetle beats his drum.
The whispers echo 'round the bend,
As night creatures start to hum.

From shadows filled with merry pranks,
The laughter rises high.
In this nurtured land of joy,
Even crickets dance and sigh.

Roots Deep in Time

With roots that link to ancient days,
The trees giggle low and deep.
They share the secrets of the past,
While wise old owls take a peep.

Beneath the sky, a riddle spins,
Of acorns spun like gold.
The stories twist and tumble,
In a playtime yet untold.

A comedy of earthy sorts,
With mushrooms clad in style.
Each ring around the trunk reveals,
A joke that makes you smile.

Roots deeper than a gossip's tale,
The forest hums with cheer.
In nature's grand, eternal play,
It's laughter we hold dear.

The Enchantment of Woodland Realms

In a forest where squirrels wear hats,
And owls hoot in whimsical chats.
The trees lean in to share a joke,
While mushrooms giggle, a laugh bespoke.

A rabbit juggles acorns with flair,
While deer prance round without a care.
They dance on leaves, a wild parade,
While the brook sings songs, a serenade.

Frogs play tunes on lily pads bright,
And fireflies twinkle, a dazzling sight.
The shadows hush as night takes its throne,
Leaving laughter to bloom, where whimsy is grown.

So wander here with a skip in your stride,
Join the woodland party, let joy be your guide.
For in this realm of mirth and cheer,
The trees hold secrets only jesters hear.

Tales from the Twisted Roots

Beneath the boughs, the stories twist,
Where tangled roots play hide and list.
A squirrel chronicles all the fights,
Of raccoons stealing snacks late at nights.

Beneath a gnarled tree, a bear takes a nap,
While ants march in single file, a map.
The wise old crow caws a gossip or two,
While critters conspire, oh what a view!

The mythical tales of gallant hamsters,
Who rode on snails through thunderstorms and banters.
Laughter erupts among the leafy crowd,
As the tales of nonsense are shared out loud.

In this realm where roots twist and play,
Chasing sunshine, and shadows sway.
A tapestry woven with giggles and gasps,
As the forest's tales shine, in humorous clasps.

Echoes of Ancient Growth

Ancient trunks whisper secrets of old,
Of mischievous sprites and treasures untold.
The wind tells tales with a playful puff,
As leaves chuckle softly, 'That's quite enough!'

The gnomes argue over who shares the best cheese,
While woodpeckers laugh, tapping rhythms with ease.
Beneath a canopy thick with splendor,
Mice make mischief—a real contender!

A chatty old vine tries to tell a fun lore,
While rabbits roll by, asking for more.
The laughter rises like bubbles in brew,
In a glen full of giggles, the antics renew.

So meet the trees with their raucous delight,
In this realm where echoes of laughter take flight.
For age brings wisdom but also a jest,
As the ancient growth plays its very best.

A Tapestry of Green Dreams

Threads of green weave dreams in the air,
Where blossoms giggle with fragrant flair.
The sun bounces through with a golden grin,
And whispers secrets, let the fun begin!

Pinecones sport ties, looking sharp and neat,
While crickets compose a whimsical beat.
The petals dance in a breezy twirl,
As butterflies join in a fluttering whirl.

Each leafy corner holds a chuckle or two,
While shadows prance about, just like you.
The laughter of flora fills every seam,
In this vibrant landscape, a whimsical dream.

So wander through wonders, where mirth reigns supreme,

In a tapestry woven of giggles and gleam.
For in this forest, where humor takes flight,
Every green dream sparkles, shining bright!

The Old Oak's Silent Stories

Beneath the boughs, the squirrels conspire,
Telling tales that never tire.
A raccoon dons a tiny crown,
While a skunk wears a silly frown.

The oak just shakes, a giggle so deep,
As the chipmunks plot, and the foxes creep.
Oh the laughter held in bark so wide,
Nature's jesters in a leafy slide.

Shadows of the Timeworn Trunk

In the shade of an ancient spine,
Lies a rabbit wearing a hat, oh so fine.
He suggests an acorn tea party soon,
But the crow thinks it's something to prune.

The shadows dance, a whimsical sight,
As the owl hoots jokes into the night.
Every leaf is an audience grand,
Laughter echoing through the land.

Forest Fables Underneath Leaves

Underneath the canopy's green,
A gopher tells tales of snacks unseen.
With a twinkle in its tiny eye,
It claims to fly, though we know it's shy.

The trees all chuckle as winds go whoosh,
While a turtle gives a slow, scoffing scoosh.
Giggles of flora fill the lush ground,
Where every creature is humor-bound.

Echoes of the Elder Grove

In the court of the wizened green,
A wise old owl feigns a queen.
With a robe of moss and a crown of vine,
He declares, "Today, we dine on pine!"

The breeze carries laughter from leaf to leaf,
As a worm tells jokes without any grief.
The laughter rings, a chorus so bright,
Echoes of joy in the fading light.

Shadows in the Forest

In the dappled shade, they dance and play,
Squirrels wear hats made of moss all day.
Owls hoot jokes with a hoity-toity flair,
While rabbits join in with a hopping hair.

The trees chuckle softly, their bark all aglow,
As critters gather to put on a show.
Raccoons in tuxedos, oh what a sight!
They serve acorn snacks till the moon's shining bright.

The wind whispers secrets that tickle the leaves,
Echoes of laughter, the forest believes.
In this leafy gather, no worry at all,
Just shadows and giggles beneath Nature's call.

Tales Told by Twisted Branches

Beneath the old oak, where tales twist and bend,
The branches gossip like a bunch of dear friends.
Acorns drop stories of summers long past,
Of dreams and mishaps that happen so fast.

A squirrel once claimed that he climbed to the sky,
But a crow cawed loudly, 'Oh, please tell me why!'
With a flick of his tail and a dash of his pride,
The squirrel just laughed, 'I was just taking a ride!'

The branches keep waving, making grand gestures,
As bunnies lean in for the best of their treasures.
With giggles and snickers, the tales dance around,
In this forest coffee shop, laughter's well-found.

The Oak's Secret Lament

Oh, dear old oak, with your limbs spread wide,
You sport a sad face that you simply can't hide.
Your leaves are all rustled; they wriggle and sway,
'What's wrong?' they all whisper, 'Is it Monday again today?'

Once you were grand, the king of the crowd,
Now you sigh deeply, not feeling so proud.
The squirrels all inch closer, a keen little bunch,
'Let's throw you a party! Come cheer up and munch!'

The acorns agree, they'll bring their best cheer,
With a sprinkle of fun, and a dash of good beer.
So the oak shakes off sorrows with a twist and a swirl,
Ready for laughter like a bright summer girl.

Wisdom in the Willows

In the willows so wise, with their long draping hair,
    They tell all the secrets that dance in the air.
'Have you heard about Bear, who danced on two feet?
    He slipped on a berry—oh, what a retreat!'

They whisper of Robin, who forgot her own tune,
    And sang to the stars every night too soon.
A fox joins the fray, with a tumble and spin,
    Claiming he's lost in a dress made of tin!

The willows chuckle, their leaves all a-quake,
    As stories of friendship and fun they awake.
With mirth in their branches, twirling around,
These wise, giggling trees make joy quite profound.

Yearning in the Underbrush

In the thicket where squirrels plot,
Acorns gossip, a nutty lot.
Branches gossip, whispering loud,
While mushrooms dance in a fuzzy shroud.

A rabbit dreams of a fancy tea,
With all his friends, just wait and see.
But the raccoon's late, his watch ran dry,
And the fox just winks, passing them by.

Beneath the ferns, a secret's kept,
Of wild adventures and squirrels who leapt.
Grumpy old owls hoot their refrain,
While frogs croak cheerfully in the rain.

Tangled roots tie tales untold,
Where the mossy treasures lie yet bold.
With giggles shared and shadows cast,
The underbrush whispers fun at last.

The Voice of the Rustling Leaves

Leaves gossip in the gentle breeze,
As critters chatter with utmost ease.
The wind just laughs, a playful tease,
Unraveling tales among the trees.

A ladybug sports a tiny hat,
While ants march by, arguing flat.
What's the best way to find a snack?
A crumb here, a crumb there—they won't turn back.

Squirrels bicker over acorn hoards,
While chipmunks dance, flinging towards.
"Not too high!" one cheeky chortles
As they tumble, creating tiny portals.

In every rustle, a joke is shared,
From tiny seeds in the branches bared.
Nature's laughter in this leafy sea,
A woodland comedy, wild and free.

Vows of the Verdant Giants

O mighty oaks with stories grand,
Swear they can dance, but never stand.
With roots entwined, a solemn pact,
To keep secrets of the forest intact.

The branches stretch, they start to sway,
While beetles join in, ready to play.
"I can bend!" claims one with flair,
"I swear I won't become a chair!"

When thunder rumbles in the sky,
They vow to flourish, reaching high.
"Not a single leaf will fall today,"
They joke, just wishing the clouds away.

With squirrels as leaders, they audibly cheer,
While chatting chipmunks spread the cheer.
In their leafy realm, humor takes flight,
Amidst the giants, oh what a sight!

Whispers of the Woodland Keeper

In twilight's glow, the keeper chuckles,
With twinkling eyes and playful knuckles.
He shuffles through the dusk-lit trees,
Playing hide-and-seek with the breeze.

"Who's hiding here?" he calls in jest,
As fireflies flicker, they join the quest.
An old raccoon winks with a grin,
"Bet you can't find where we've all been!"

The shadows twist in secret dance,
While fawns peek out, quick to prance.
"Let's spin a tale," they all agree,
In the keeper's realm, where joy flows free.

Each rustle holds a laugh in store,
As stories echo forevermore.
With bramble thickets and starlit skies,
The woodland keeper spreads delight, oh my!

Legends of the Woodland Sentinel

In the grove where shadows laugh,
A tree wears green with pride and glee.
Birds gossip round the bark's soft staff,
Telling tales of squirrels, wild and free.

Once, a deer thought it could dance,
Tripped on roots, it took a fall.
The oak chuckled at the chance,
As acorns rolled, it laughed with all.

Rabbits gather for a grand old toast,
To celebrate the oak's wise eyes.
They claim it's seen all, coast to coast,
While munching clover, oh, how time flies!

With every breeze, the branches sway,
And whisper secrets from the past.
A wise old oak, in its goofy way,
Watches over tales that forever last.

Nature's Heartbeat in the Stillness

Beneath the branches, stories bloom,
Of critters near the mossy seat.
A chipmunk found a cozy room,
And threw a party—what a treat!

The owls hoot in a funny choir,
Competing with the rustling leaves.
A dance-off sparks a wild desire,
As chipmunks sway and shake with ease.

The sun peeks through, a shiny guide,
A rabbit's wiggle draws a cheer.
The forest laughs with joy and pride,
As nature's heartbeat draws us near.

With each tick and tock of the day,
The woodland giggles, what a sound!
In this green haven, come what may,
Laughter and light will abound!

Caresses of Time on Mossy Shoulders

On mossy shoulders, wisdom rests,
With time's soft touch, a gentle nudge.
The old oak chuckles at the jest,
As lichens bloom, they form a grudge.

Once a squirrel claimed it had found,
A treasure trove beneath a cone.
Yet starlit nights, it spun around,
And lost the route back to its home.

A fox strolled by with a knowing grin,
As if to say, 'Oh, not again!'
The oak just swayed, with such a spin,
"Those younglings never learn, Amen!"

With laughter echoing through the trees,
Time tickles roots and wiggles leaves,
In each embrace, we feel the breeze,
And share the joy that nature weaves.

Parables from the Old Growth

In a forest thick, with tales to tell,
An oak stands tall, a jester wise.
It knows that life is a funny spell,
Where mushrooms dance and shadows rise.

Squirrels plot their heist of nuts,
While crows critique from branches high.
An acorn falls, it giggles, 'What's
A little mishap in a world so spry?'

The deer in stripes misread the game,
Too busy posing in the clear.
The oak just shakes, not one to blame,
And cheers them on with a knowing cheer.

With every bark, a giggle swells,
A lesson wrapped in playful glee.
From ancient roots where laughter dwells,
The forest whispers, 'Come play with me!'

Where Shadows Embrace the Earth

In a forest where odd things sway,
Leaves chatter gossip in bright array.
A squirrel wears socks; it's quite a sight,
As the sun giggles,   tickling the night.

A deer with a hat struts down the path,
While rabbits debate who's got the best math.
The tree's got a smile, it's hard to ignore,
It whispers, "Hey, let's invite some more!"

The owls in glasses are reading a book,
Beneath branches that sway, the leaves gently shook.
The mushrooms are dancing—what a wild ball,
Who knew the woods were a carnival?

So when you wander down this cheerful way,
Join in the fun; don't just look and stay.
Where shadows embrace and laughter's a friend,
In this whimsical realm, the good times won't end.

Roots of Reverie in Saturated Soil

In a bog where the giggles bloom brightly,
Toads wear tuxedos, but it's not quite rightly.
The frogs sing duets in a slippery style,
While snails with monocles study for a while.

The lilies take naps on a fluffy white bed,
As crickets discuss what the frogs might have said.
A raccoon with swagger holds court on a rock,
And everyone laughs at the clock that won't talk.

Beneath mossy hats, the secrets are sprawled,
Each root a storyteller, proud and enthralled.
The mud gives a chuckle, as breezes arise,
With mirth in the air, beneath half-open skies.

If you wish to glimpse where the playful heads meet,
In roots of reveries, oh what a treat!
Embrace all the silliness, let spirits uncoil,
In the magic that bubbles from saturated soil.

Whispers Beneath the Canopy

Beneath leafy arches, the jokes fly so fast,
A chattering chipmunk recaps the past.
The wind throws a pun, rustling leaves with flair,
While the ants throw confetti and dance without care.

A tree with a beak starts chirping a tune,
And squirrels are juggling acorns 'neath the moon.
The giants of wood stand, boasting in cheer,
'Tis a comedy heaven we find here, my dear.

When shadows get long and the night starts to crawl,
A band of raccoons puts on a grand ball.
With moonlight as spotlight, they sing and they spin,
In whispers of laughter, adventures begin.

So tread lightly, friend, where the giggles abound,
In the canopy's heart, joy is ever found.
From the roots to the tips, let your spirits ignite,
In this woodland of whimsy, where day feels like night.

Secrets of the Ancient Grove

In a grove where the old trees play twists and turns,
Laughter erupts from the mossy concerns.
The termites host parties with crumbs as their prize,
While the worms gossip softly, disguised in their lies.

A hedgehog in boots leads a parade of the proud,
While ferrets perform under clouds that are loud.
Each critter has something to cheerfully say,
In a dance of delight, they frolic and sway.

The rocks are debating the best spots to nap,
While bunnies are plotting a matchmaking rap.
The owls sit perched, like wise judges on high,
With quips full of humor as they watch the sky.

So wander, dear friend, in this lively old place,
Where secrets and laughter twirl with such grace.
In the ancient grove, the stories will flow,
In the heart of the woods, let your joy overflow.

Underneath an Age-Old Canopy

Beneath the branches, squirrels debate,
Acorns tossed like a wild state.
Who can gather the most today?
While chattering birds cheer them on, hooray!

A raccoon plots a daring heist,
While mice munch on cakes, not once but thrice.
The old tree chuckles and sways,
As nature's jesters steal the day.

Beneath the shade, insects prance,
Crickets chirp in a zany dance.
Each leaf a stage for antics bold,
Nature's comedy, a sight to behold!

And as the sun dips low tonight,
The canopy glows in fading light.
With laughter echoing through the wood,
The age-old tree feels quite understood.

Hidden Histories in Nature's Lap

Under the roots, secrets lie,
Tales of mischief, oh my, oh my!
A family of owls hoots with glee,
Sharing stories of grand-squirrel spree.

A lost shoe, a picnic's fate,
The ants feasting on crumbs, it's great!
Beetles roll their tiny bales,
While frogs croak out forgotten tales.

A wise old frog, with nothing but pride,
Claims to have seen the moon take a ride.
The chatter grows, with gossip so wild,
Nature's lap, where humor's compiled!

In the hush of dusk, the stories blend,
Hidden histories that never end.
With each rustle, a laugh takes flight,
Under the stars, everything feels right.

Timeless Whispers of the Forest

Whispers float on a breeze so bright,
Tales of critters in day and night.
The wise old tree, it knows them all,
From rambunctious raccoons to a skink's small crawl.

"Mice play chess," it rustles low,
"While rabbits hop, fast and slow!"
The forest giggles with every sound,
A happy symphony all around.

Leafy whispers tell of a dance,
As butterflies twirl in a summer trance.
The wild things swing and twine so free,
In the timeless laughter of you and me.

So if you pause and listen deep,
The forest holds joy, its secrets keep.
In every shade and soft moonlight,
Lies a giggle, just out of sight.

The Guardian of Twisted Trunks

With limbs that twist like a jester's grin,
The old oak stands where tales begin.
Squirrels mimic the shape of its bark,
Gathering tales until it's dark.

Frogs lurk low on the branches wide,
Planning an opera, full of pride.
With each croak, a note in the air,
The guardian chuckles, unaware.

Raccoons wear masks as they creep and crawl,
Taunting the owl who's regal and tall.
Under the moon, their games ignite,
While the twisted trunk holds laughter tight.

With roots entwined, the laughter grows,
As night unveils its playful shows.
In the heart of the woods, so full of cheer,
A guardian reigns, forever near.

In Praise of the Beautiful Canopy

Up high the branches sway with glee,
Dancing like a party, you see!
Acorns drop like surprise confetti,
Squirrels snicker – it's all very petty.

A hat for the birds, a stage for the bees,
A wonderland woven with ticklish leaves.
Why do they laugh, under skies so blue?
No one knows why, but it tickles them too!

Mighty limbs arch like ancient fables,
Offering tales that twist like cables.
Beneath its shade, we share our treats,
Maybe it's magic, or just clever feats!

So here's to the canopy, grand and spry,
Where secrets whisper and giggles fly.
Nature's own theater, a sight to behold,
Bring snacks and a chair, and let the fun unfold!

Secrets of the Rooted Ones

Deep in the soil, the roots start to plot,
Making up games that get pretty hot.
"Who can tickle the ground the most?"
"Let's start a rooting good ghost!"

They wriggle and giggle, a hidden delight,
Tickling beetles, oh what a sight!
"Join us!" they call from under the grass,
"You'll never out-funny these roots, you lass!"

But little do they know of our schemes,
We cheat with worms, or so it seems.
They think they're the jesters, the kings of the land,
But wait till we spill our giggles and stand!

Well-rooted in laughter, mischievous and bold,
Their secrets we keep, a tale to be told.
Next time you're strolling, don't trip or fuss,
Just know the roots are all laughing at us!

Enchantment of the Elder Grove

In the groovy glade, the elders convene,
With tales of the past that are rarely seen.
"Remember that time when the wind gave a shove?"
"Ha! Even trees need a good shove of love!"

They chuckle and creak, the wisdom is pure,
Mossy old sages with laughter demure.
Branches like arms, waving in jest,
Fungi all giggling at an acorn's request!

Echoes of pranks linger in the air,
"Who painted the bark? Was it Fred or Claire?"
They roll their bark eyes, for the tales never end,
In the elder grove, every tree is a friend.

So stroll through the shade with a grin on your face,
Sway with the whispers, join in on the chase.
For in the old grove, where legends are spun,
A good hearty laugh makes the aging fun!

Flickers of Forgotten Hues

As twilight dances in hues quite rare,
The trees shimmy their leaves with flair.
Colors emerge like a vibrant crew,
Glowing like fireflies in a curious zoo.

"Is that yellow? Wait, is that blue?"
"Who's dressing up? Oh, is it you?"
The shades have a soiree, attire ludicrous,
Even the shadows are joining, how curious!

"Stand tall," whispers red, "and don't be shy",
"Let's show leafy laughter beneath the sky!"
Each flicker, a jest, from roots to the crown,
They twirl and they twirl, in a leafy gown.

So embrace the shift with quirks and charms,
Nature invites us with open arms.
In every shade, a tale unfolds,
Of laughter and whimsy, timeless as gold!

Stories Woven in Woodland Silence

In a forest deep where whispers dance,
A squirrel pranced in a shiny pants.
The trees all giggled, their branches shook,
While a rabbit read from a dusty book.

A fox wore glasses, so wise and sage,
He gave advice but forgot his age.
The owl hooted jokes, with a wink in eye,
'Trust me,' he said, 'I can really fly!'

A deer told tales of a pie so grand,
Baked with berries picked by each tiny hand.
The forest chuckled, alive with glee,
As animals laughed, 'Join the jamboree!'

So wander through where the giggles grow,
In a hush of green, let the laughter flow.
Each tree a witness, all branches sway,
In woodland wonders where fun holds sway.

Messages in the Mossy Shadows

In the shadows green, where the moss does thrive,
A raccoon sent memos, quite the archive.
With tiny glasses and a pen of twigs,
He wrote down secrets of all woodland digs.

A turtle, slow, with a cap on his head,
Claimed he was faster than all of the spread.
But when it came time for a race on the path,
He tripped on a root, oh, the aftermath!

The chipmunks debated trees' silly names,
Like 'Franklin the Fluffy' and 'Timmy's Games.'
Each whispered secret wrapped soft in the night,
Mossy shadows gleamed with curious light.

Beneath the branches, the whispers took flight,
With giggles and stories that danced through the night.
In the mossy embrace, every chuckle does grow,
As shadows share secrets, both high and low.

Reflections of the Revered Oak

Oh, mighty oak with branches so wide,
You've seen it all, the forest pride.
With acorns falling like little rain,
You chuckle softly — are you quite sane?

The mice hold court on your wooden throne,
With cheese and bread, they sing and groan.
In debates they argue, of cheese or cracker,
Only to pause, when the baker's backer!

A beetle once claimed he could fly the moon,
But tripped on a leaf and fell down in tune.
The oak just laughed, 'You'll need wings, my friend!'
And thus began tales that would never end.

Reflections glimmer in golden light,
As creatures gather to share in delight.
With roots in laughter and branches in glee,
The revered one reigns, our jester so free.

The Lure of the Leafy Labyrinth

In a maze of leaves where the laughter grows,
The gnomes whisper riddles beneath the toes.
A wandering fox with a map upside down,
Claimed he was king; all laughed in the town.

A hedgehog dressed smart in a tiny bow tie,
Conducted the orchestra, oh my oh my!
With crickets a-singing and frogs gone astray,
The leaf-carpeted dance stole the bright day.

The paths twisted round like a playful breeze,
And wisps of the forest begged one to tease.
But getting lost was the sweetest delight,
In the leafy labyrinth of joy and light.

So prance through the maze where the giggles reside,
And join the festivities, don't let them slide.
For in every turn and every soft bend,
The lure of laughter is yours to fend.

Chronicles of the Gnarled Trunk

In the forest stood a tree, so wise and old,
With branches that twisted like stories told.
Squirrels would chatter, their gossip so grand,
While raccoons debated, a critter band.

The trunk boasted wrinkles, like hands of a sage,
Whispering secrets, each twist an age.
A bird on the branch wore a cap and specs,
Claiming to teach all the woodland Rex!

Bees buzzed around, a confused little swarm,
Claiming the honey was part of their charm.
But the tree just chuckled, bark shaking with mirth,
How much mischief could spring from the earth?

So if you stroll by, lend an ear to the tale,
Of the humorous trunk who could never grow stale.
With laughter and giggles, the forest would cheer,
For the gnarled old trunk brought them all near.

Essence of the Evergreens

In a patch of green, the pines stood so tall,
With needles that tickled, they teased one and all.
One pine said, "Friends, let's throw a grand feast!"
And soon there was dancing, from the greatest to least.

A hedgehog with style wore a hat made of spruce,
Claiming it fresh and a bit of a moose.
The owls hooted tunes, but not quite in tune,
While rabbits just hopped, as if on a balloon.

The squirrel was a chef, with acorns on hand,
Whipping up dishes that no one could stand.
"Be careful," said badger, "that stew's quite a risk!
Last time it exploded, we lost the whole brisk!"

Yet laughter erupted, as night turned to morn,
With stories of fun, and three-legged corn.
Amongst evergreens tall, all worries took flight,
In the essence of jests, all felt just right.

The Heartbeat of the Forest

Deep in the woods, where shadows do play,
The trees all breathed life, in their own funny way.
A crow with a cackle, a real card to boot,
Claimed laughter was nature's most charming pursuit.

The fox in the thicket wore shoes made of leaves,
Said, "Dancing is easy, just follow your eaves!"
While raccoons in suits held a fine dinner chat,
Discussing the merits of stylish top hats.

A single old acorn rolled down with a clunk,
Proclaiming, "I'm destined to be quite the funk!"
So the critters all gathered, they shimmied and swayed,
Rejoicing in dance till the sun started to fade.

And the heartbeat of laughter, they felt deep inside,
Rang out through the forest, the pride they could't hide.
With jokes on the breeze, all worries were lost,
For the woods' merry pulse, no price could be cost.

Starlight in the Oak's Embrace

Under a sky where the fireflies waltz,
A grand oak stood proud with no thought of faults.
"Come gather, come linger!" the branches all said,
"We'll share all the tales that we've crafted and bred!"

The glow of the moon cast a comical light,
As raccoons wore sunglasses, thinking they're bright.
The owls chimed in with their wisecracks and puns,
"Why don't scientists trust atoms?" they run!

The crickets were concerting, a riotous tune,
Twirling the jokes 'round till they danced with the moon.
The old oak just chuckled, its leaves in a swirl,
As critters debated who twirled like a girl:

So remember the starlight, the laughter in trees,
Where critters held court under canopies' ease.
In the oak's warm embrace, fun never runs dry,
With joy in the forest, where chuckles fly high!

The Legacy of the Leafy Canopy

In whispers of green, the branches sway,
Leaves giggle softly, brightening the day.
Old acorns chuckle, tucked safe in the bark,
As squirrels throw parties from dawn until dark.

The roots tell tales of the friends that they knew,
With each tickle of grass, the laughter just grew.
Even the nests share a quirky refrain,
Of birds who complain when it starts to rain.

Sunbeams will prance through the canopy high,
While critters below just bask and sigh.
In this leafy hall, the fun never ends,
Where laughter and nature are always good friends.

So raise up a cheer for the grandest of trees,
With its leafy delights and rustling leaves.
In shadows and sunlight, they dance all around,
A legacy grand, where joy can be found.

Odes to the Obscured Glade

In the glade that's hidden, where humor flows bright,
The rabbits wear hats, what a curious sight!
With whispers of mischief and giggles around,
The secrets they share, oh so slyly profound.

The mushrooms hold court with the bugs that they host,
While crickets recite poetry, toasting with toast.
Each flower a jester, each leaf a grand player,
In this glorious space, a nature's own frayer.

The dancing of shadows, a waltz on the floor,
Where squirrels turn cartwheels, and pinecones explore.
Every twig quivers with laughter and cheer,
A spectacle rare, oh so wondrously clear!

So come one, come all, to the glade out of sight,
Where laughter's the compass, and all feels just right.
In the embrace of the trees, let your worries abate,
For joy in the glade is a magical state.

Secrets in the Shade

Under the broad arms of a wise, old tree,
The secrets of nature swirl happily.
With the rustle of leaves, a joke on the breeze,
And laughter that settles like dust on the knees.

The shadows play tag with the sun's golden rays,
While the critters concoct their whimsical ways.
Frogs in top hats go leaping around,
While beetles fly past with a five-star sound.

In burrows and nooks, tales of wonder are spun,
Of raccoons' cabarets where the fun has begun.
Each giggle and chuckle, a note of delight,
A chorus of nature, both merry and bright.

So find your way here, where the silliness reigns,
In the shade of the wisdom, where no one complains.
Layered in laughter, with whispers anew,
The secrets in shade are awaiting for you.

The Guardian of Forgotten Paths

A gnarled old tree stands with a grin on its face,
Guarding the trails of this mystical place.
With knots like a smile and leaves full of jest,
It shelters the fun-loving critters, no less.

Overgrown vines curl like fingers of fate,
Inviting the wanderers, don't hesitate!
With stories from saplings that bounce through the air,
While hedgehogs and badgers parade without care.

As echoes of laughter dance through the glade,
And shadows play tricks with each move that they made.
Underneath branches that sway to the beat,
The guardian chuckles, "Now isn't this sweet?"

So grab your bold heart and stroll down the lane,
Where whimsy and wonder are never in vain.
A guardian steadfast, in laughter it bathes,
Keeping the magic alive in the swathes.

Langue of the Leaves

In the grove where whispers dwell,
Leaves have secrets just to tell.
They chatter loud when breezes pass,
Gossiping 'bout the squirrel's sass.

One leaf claims it wore a crown,
While another just fell down.
A twig interrupts with snickers bright,
"Don't listen, friend, they're full of fright!"

The acorns chuckle as they roll,
"Who's the king? We'll take a poll!"
A rustling voice, in high demand,
"Guilty as charged! I ate that bran!"

So if you sneak and take a peek,
The leaves will giggle—what a sneak!
Join their chimes, hear their delight,
In their jests, the day feels bright.

Whispers through the Wild

In the wild where shadows play,
Tiny creatures dance and sway.
A rabbit hops with a wink and grin,
"Did you hear about the fox's spin?"

The owls hoot in a friendly quirk,
Sharing tales of the doggone perk.
A hen squawks, "That's downright nutty!"
As the tortoise shouts, "Oh, isn't it cutty!"

The trees lean in, their boughs all twist,
To catch each jest, they cannot resist!
Mice tweet gossip, they nod and cheer,
"Is it true that the cat's got fear?"

So wander through this living spree,
Where every word is a jubilee.
For in the wild, each secret barks,
You'll find the laughter lit with sparks.

The Spirits of Shady Realms

In shady realms where spirits play,
They pour their laughs by night and day.
A ghostly sage in a leafy cloak,
Whispers, "Life's a funny joke!"

The mushrooms giggle as they sway,
"Look at us—who's the fun guy, hey?"
A fox trots past, with a knowing glee,
"Tell me more, this mustn't be!"

The shadows dance, and the crickets cheer,
"Join the party, do not fear!"
They prance around the ancient roots,
Where every laugh just simply boosts.

So breathe in deep, this jest-filled air,
Let every chuckle ease your care.
For in the shade, in realms divine,
The spirits laugh, and all is fine.

Echoing through the Forest's Heart

In the forest's cozy heart,
Echoes play a lively part.
A deer prances, laughing loud,
"Was that a twig? Or just a cloud?"

Beneath the boughs, a party brews,
With raccoons in their silly shoes.
They trade their hats and swipe a pie,
"Let's steal some food! Oh me, oh my!"

The brook giggles with bubbling joy,
As a frog leaps, a cheeky boy.
"Did you catch that silly fish?
Oh never mind, I'll grant a wish!"

So wander forth, let laughter lead,
In every rustle, there's a seed.
For in the heart where echoes play,
Funny tales will save the day.

A Tapestry of Twisting Branches

In the forest where whispers croon,
Branches twist like dance in the moon.
Squirrels argue over acorn treats,
While shadows leap on tiny feet.

A knotty limb plays peek-a-boo,
With a raccoon wearing a sun hat too.
Together they giggle, oh what a scene!
As birds get tangled in branches, it seems.

Old tree's got jokes, it wobbles and sways,
A stand-up act in the woods that pays.
Laughing sap drips down to the ground,
While the fox rolls over, laughter abound.

So come hither, join in the fun,
Among this leafy, leafy run.
With nature's antics, life is a jest,
All under the boughs, we are all blessed.

The Lore of the Leafy Sentinel

Once there stood a quirky tree,
With branches that tickled, oh so free.
This leafy giant, wise and grand,
Gave sage advice at a woodland band.

Squirrels in ties play cards at dusk,
While owls hoot riddles, oh what a fuss!
A turtle in shades, nonchalant and cool,
Dances in circles, breaking the rule.

"Don't hug too tight!" the tree would bark,
"It tickles my bark, like a funny lark!"
Then all would giggle till stars came out,
In this forest of fun, there's never a doubt.

So heed the tales that the leaves shall share,
Of laughter and joy, floating through air.
Join the revel, oh don't be shy,
Under the chuckling limbs, let's all fly!

Chronicles of the Woodland Watcher

In a glade where the most curious things play,
A tree stands guard, through night and day.
With eyes of moss, it surveys the scene,
Chasing bunnies with a giggle, so keen.

The birds gossip while hiding in twigs,
Telling tales of the forest's jigs.
A porcupine prances, uncommonly brisk,
While a disco ball drops, oh what a risk!

"Keep your dance moves, oh so spry!"
Crows cackle loudly, "Don't let them fly!"
Here in the woods, the antics don't cease,
With laughter and joy, they find their peace.

So gather around, let's share a cheer,
Under the watchful boughs, wipe away fear.
For nature's the stage, with a whimsical twist,
In this woodland tale, joy can't be missed!

In the Embrace of Gnarled Limbs

Gnarled limbs like fingers, reaching for fun,
In this wild world, laughter's never done.
A chattering chipmunk, picking his nose,
While a wise old owl tells jokes in prose.

Frogs croak a tune, like a jazz band's delight,
As crickets keep time under the moonlight.
With furry friends, they convene and meet,
For snacks of berries and a rhythm so sweet.

"Hey there, tree!" a squirrel doth shout,
"Is it your turn to wiggle about?"
And with every rustle and bounce, there's a cheer,
For the best kind of gatherings happen right here!

So sway with the branches, let giggles unfold,
In the arms of this tree, watch each story told.
In the embrace, where joy intertwines,
Nature holds us close, in her playful designs!

The Compass in the Canopy

A squirrel once sought out a map,
In branches he had a little nap.
He woke up lost, oh such a plight,
Thinking acorns could lead him right.

The compass spun, oh what a fuss,
Pointing north, then south—what's the fuss?
With every twitch, he lost his cheer,
And blamed it all on that pesky deer.

So high he climbed, with all his flair,
Over leaves and through light air.
He found a nut! A great big score,
But it turned out to be a pinecone, for sure!

Now he tells tales of his grand quest,
To find a compass that never rests.
Though weary he climbs, he feels no shame,
For every nut lost was just a game!

Spirits of the Woodland Whisper

In shadows deep where whispers creep,
The spirits giggle, oh, what a peep!
They rise at dusk, wear gowns of leaves,
And tease the deer who hardly believes.

With whoops and howls, they dance and sway,
While owls cast glances, thinking, 'What a day!'
One sprightly sprite tripped on a vine,
And landed square, oh ain't that fine!

'Twas a raccoon who rolled with glee,
Watching spirits sip herbal tea.
They clink their cups in the moon's shine,
Bubbling laughter, oh how divine!

But come the dawn, the mischief fades,
Into the trees where their fun parades.
Yet when night falls, they reappear,
With swirling giggles, joy and Cheer!

Enigma among the Elders

Among the wise oaks, secrets gather,
A riddle is born, it's light as a feather.
Squirrels ponder, 'What do they eat?'
While birds complain, 'This mystery's sweet!'

The owls hoot, 'A dilemma unsolved!'
As the forest's conundrum slowly evolved.
Would they solve it on a sunny day,
Or in shadowy depths where the critters play?

One raccoon said, 'Let's follow the trails,'
And off they dashed like adorable snails.
A glance at the oaks, a twitch of the nose,
They all agreed; no one really knows!

Yet laughter rang clear, so sweet and bright,
As friends sought the answers within the night.
With giggles and snacks, the puzzle unspooled,
It's better to laugh than to feel like a fool!

The Solace of Swaying Branches

On breezy days, the branches sway,
A dance so silly, they steal the play.
A brave little bird took a dizzy flight,
And landed with splat! It gave them a fright!

Chirps turned to chuckles, the scene was set,
As the branches waved with no hint of regret.
The bird fluffed feathers and gave a smirk,
'Best landing ever, now that's a perk!'

The trees held secrets, oh so dear,
With rustles and tickles that drew them near.
They whispered tales of a million shrieks,
Of raccoons stealing snacks—those cheeky freaks!

In every sway, there's comfort found,
And laughter thrums in the playful ground.
So join the dance, let worries slip,
In the solace of branches, we take a dip!

www.ingramcontent.com/pod-product-compliance
Lightning Source LLC
Chambersburg PA
CBHW072147200426
43209CB00051B/812